Tattoo
Journal and Sketchbook

By Gangie Marie and Cameron Purvis

Be Amazing, LLC Publishing
Youngsville, Louisiana
First Edition, November 2020

Copyright © mmxx Be Amazing, LLC Publishing Not to be reproduced.

Text Copyright © 2020 by Tangie Marie ®
Illustrations Copyright © 2020 by Cameron Purvis and
Illustrations Copyright © 2020 by Tangie Marie ®
Tattoo Journal and Sketchbook characters, names and related indicia
are trademarks of and © Be Amazing, LLC by Tangie Marie ®
owned and operated by Tangie Purvis

All rights reserved.
Published by Be Amazing, LLC Publishing, Youngsville, Louisiana
The publisher does not have any control over and does not assume
any responsibility for author or third-party websites or their content.
Tattoo Journal and Sketchbook publishing rights Be Amazing, LLC
No part of this publication may be reproduced, stored in a retrieval system,
or transmitted in any form or by any means, electronic, mechanical,
photocopying, recording, or otherwise, without written permission
of the publisher. The Tattoo Journal and Sketchbook is intended for
inspirational and personal use only. No part of this Tattoo Journal
and Sketchbook can be used for commercial purposes without prior consent.
For information regarding permission, email Be Amazing, LLC by Tangie Marie ®
Attention: Permissions Department, Be Amazing Golden Headquarters,
info@tangiemarie.com

Names, characters, places, and incidents are either the product of the
author's imagination or are used fictitiously, and any resemblance to
actual persons, living or dead, business establishments, events or locales
is entirely coincidental.

ISBN 978-1-7360796-0-7 (Paperback)

Be Amazing, LLC Publishing
Youngsville, Louisiana
First Edition, November 2020

This Tattoo Journal and Sketchbook
Belongs To:

_____

Tattoo Journal and Sketchbook Table of Contents

Project Title	Page (s)

Tattoo Journal and Sketchbook Table of Contents

Project Title	Page (s)

Copyright © mmxx Be Amazing, LLC Publishing. Not to be reproduced.

Tattoo Journal and Sketchbook Table of Contents

Project Title	Page(s)

Copyright © mmxx Be Amazing, LLC Publishing. Not to be reproduced.

Tattoo Journal and Sketchbook Table of Contents

Project Title	Page(s)

Copyright © mmxx Be Amazing, LLC Publishing. Not to be reproduced.

Client Name:

Placement:

Theme:

Planned Date:

Palette

Design:

Details / Notes:

Copyright © mmxx Be Amazing LLC Publishing. Not to be reproduced.

Name _____ Date _____

Half Sleeve Sketch Template

Copyright © mmxx Be Amazing, LLC Publishing. Not to be reproduced.

Client Name:

Placement:

Theme:

Planned Date:

Palette

Design:

Details / Notes:

Copyright © mmxx Be Amazing, LLC Publishing. Not to be reproduced.

Name _____ Date _____

Half Sleeve Sketch Template

Copyright © mmxx Be Amazing, LLC Publishing. Not to be reproduced.

Client Name:

Placement:

Theme:

Planned Date:

Palette

Design:

Details / Notes:

Copyright © mmxx Be Amazing, LLC Publishing Not to be reproduced.

Name _____ Date _____

Half Sleeve Sketch Template

Copyright © mmxx Be Amazing, LLC Publishing Not to be reproduced.

Client Name:

Placement:

Theme:

Planned Date:

Palette

Design:

Details / Notes:

Copyright © mmxx Be Amazing, LLC Publishing Not to be reproduced.

Name _____ Date _____

Half Sleeve Sketch Template

Copyright © mmxx Be Amazing, LLC Publishing. Not to be reproduced.

Client Name:

Placement:

Theme:

Planned Date:

Palette

Design:

Details / Notes:

Name _____ Date _____

Half Sleeve Sketch Template

Copyright © mmxx Be Amazing, LLC Publishing Not to be reproduced.

Client Name:

Placement:

Theme:

Planned Date:

Palette

Design:

Details / Notes:

Copyright © mmxx Be Amazing, LLC Publishing. Not to be reproduced.

Name _____ Date _____

Half Sleeve Sketch Template

Copyright © mmxx Be Amazing, LLC Publishing. Not to be reproduced.

Client Name:

Placement:

Theme:

Planned Date:

Palette

Design:

Details / Notes:

Copyright © mmxx Be Amazing, LLC Publishing. Not to be reproduced.

Name _____   Date _____

Half Sleeve Sketch Template

Copyright © mmxx Be Amazing, LLC Publishing Not to be reproduced.

Client Name:

Placement:

Theme:

Planned Date:

Palette

Design:

Details / Notes:

Copyright © mmxx Be Amazing, LLC Publishing. Not to be reproduced.

Name _____ Date _____

Half Sleeve Sketch Template

Copyright © mmxx Be Amazing, LLC Publishing. Not to be reproduced.

Client Name:

Placement:

Theme:

Planned Date:

Palette

Design:

Details / Notes:

Copyright © mmxx Be Amazing, LLC Publishing. Not to be reproduced.

Name _____ Date _____

Half Sleeve Sketch Template

Copyright © mmxx Be Amazing, LLC Publishing. Not to be reproduced.

Client Name:

Placement:

Theme:

Planned Date:

Palette

Design:

Details / Notes:

Copyright © mmxx Be Amazing, LLC Publishing. Not to be reproduced.

Name _____ Date _____

Half Sleeve Sketch Template

Copyright © mmxx Be Amazing, LLC Publishing. Not to be reproduced.

Client Name:

Placement:

Theme:

Planned Date:

Palette

Design:

Details / Notes: _____

Copyright © mmxx Be Amazing, LLC Publishing. Not to be reproduced.

Name _____ Date _____

Half Sleeve Sketch Template

Copyright © mmxx Be Amazing, LLC Publishing Not to be reproduced.

Client Name:

Placement:

Theme:

Planned Date:

Palette

Design:

Details / Notes: _____

Copyright © mmxx Be Amazing, LLC Publishing. Not to be reproduced.

Name _____ Date _____

Half Sleeve Sketch Template

Copyright © mmxx Be Amazing, LLC Publishing. Not to be reproduced.

Client Name:

Placement:

Theme:

Planned Date:

Palette

Design:

Details / Notes:

Copyright © mmxx Be Amazing, LLC Publishing. Not to be reproduced.

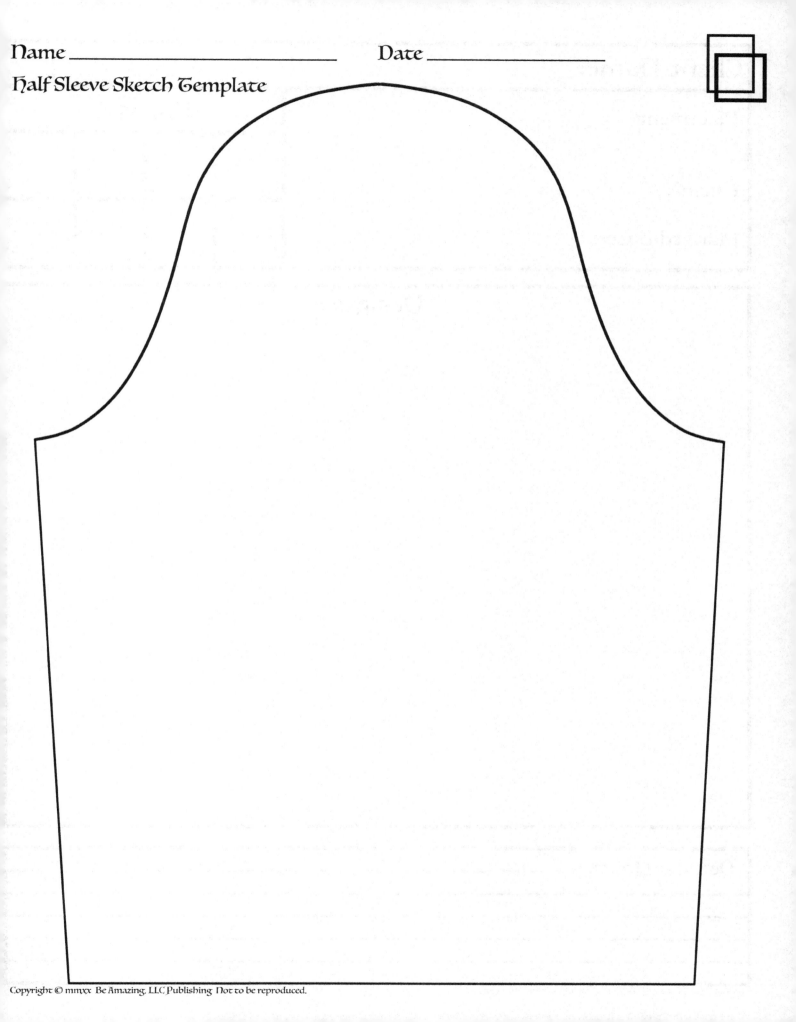

Client Name:

Placement:

Theme:

Planned Date:

Palette

Design:

Details / Notes:

Copyright © mmxx Be Amazing, LLC Publishing. Not to be reproduced.

Name _____ Date _____

Half Sleeve Sketch Template

Copyright © mmxx Be Amazing, LLC Publishing. Not to be reproduced.

Client Name:

Placement:

Theme:

Planned Date:

Palette

Design:

Details / Notes:

Name _____ Date _____

Half Sleeve Sketch Template

Copyright © mmxx Be Amazing, LLC Publishing. Not to be reproduced.

Client Name:

Placement:

Theme:

Planned Date:

Palette

Design:

Details / Notes:

Copyright © mmxx Be Amazing, LLC Publishing. Not to be reproduced.

Name _____ Date _____

Half Sleeve Sketch Template

Copyright © mmxx Be Amazing, LLC Publishing. Not to be reproduced.

Client Name:

Placement:

Theme:

Planned Date:

Palette

Design:

Details / Notes:

Name _____   Date _____

Half Sleeve Sketch Template

Copyright © mmxx Be Amazing, LLC Publishing. Not to be reproduced.

Client Name:

Placement:

Theme:

Planned Date:

Palette

Design:

Details / Notes:

Copyright © mmxx Be Amazing, LLC Publishing. Not to be reproduced.

Name _____ Date _____

Half Sleeve Sketch Template

Copyright © mmxx Be Amazing, LLC Publishing. Not to be reproduced.

Client Name:

Placement:

Theme:

Planned Date:

Palette

Design:

Details/Notes:

Copyright © mmxx Be Amazing, LLC Publishing. Not to be reproduced.

Name _____ Date _____

Half Sleeve Sketch Template

Copyright © mmxx Be Amazing, LLC Publishing. Not to be reproduced.

Client Name:

Placement:

Theme:

Planned Date:

Palette

Design:

Details / Notes:

Copyright © mmxx Be Amazing, LLC Publishing. Not to be reproduced.

Name _____ Date _____

Half Sleeve Sketch Template

Copyright © mmxx Be Amazing, LLC Publishing. Not to be reproduced.

Client Name:

Placement:

Theme:

Planned Date:

Palette

Design:

Details / Notes:

Copyright © mmxx Be Amazing, LLC Publishing. Not to be reproduced.

Name _____ Date _____

Half Sleeve Sketch Template

Copyright © mmxx Be Amazing, LLC Publishing. Not to be reproduced.

Client Name:

Placement:

Theme:

Planned Date:

Palette

Design:

Details / Notes:

Copyright © mmxx Be Amazing, LLC Publishing. Not to be reproduced.

Name _____ Date _____

Half Sleeve Sketch Template

Copyright © mmxx Be Amazing, LLC Publishing Not to be reproduced.

Client Name:

Placement:

Theme:

Planned Date:

Palette

Design:

Details / Notes:

Copyright © mmxx Be Amazing, LLC Publishing. Not to be reproduced.

Name _____ Date _____

Half Sleeve Sketch Template

Copyright © mmxx Be Amazing, LLC Publishing. Not to be reproduced.

Client Name:

Placement:

Theme:

Planned Date:

Palette

Design:

Details / Notes:

Copyright © mmxx Be Amazing, LLC Publishing. Not to be reproduced.

Name _____ Date _____

Half Sleeve Sketch Template

Copyright © mmxx Be Amazing, LLC Publishing Not to be reproduced.

Client Name:

Placement:

Theme:

Planned Date:

Palette

Design:

Details / Notes:

Copyright © mmxx Be Amazing, LLC Publishing. Not to be reproduced.

Name _____ Date _____

Half Sleeve Sketch Template

Copyright © mmxx Be Amazing, LLC Publishing. Not to be reproduced.

Client Name:

Placement:

Theme:

Planned Date:

Palette

Design:

Details / Notes: _____

Copyright © mmxx Be Amazing, LLC Publishing. Not to be reproduced.

Name _____ Date _____
Forearm Sketch Template

Copyright © mmxx Be Amazing, LLC Publishing. Not to be reproduced.

Client Name:

Placement:

Theme:

Planned Date:

Palette

Design:

Details / Notes:

Copyright © mmxx Be Amazing, LLC Publishing. Not to be reproduced.

Name _____ Date _____
Forearm Sketch Template

Copyright © mmxx Be Amazing, LLC Publishing. Not to be reproduced.

Client Name:

Placement:

Theme:

Planned Date:

Palette

Design:

Details / Notes:

Copyright © mmxx Be Amazing, LLC Publishing. Not to be reproduced.

Name _____ Date _____
Forearm Sketch Template

Copyright © mmxx Be Amazing, LLC Publishing. Not to be reproduced.

Client Name:

Placement:

Theme:

Planned Date:

Palette

Design:

Details / Notes: _____

Copyright © mmxx Be Amazing, LLC Publishing. Not to be reproduced.

Name _____ Date _____
Forearm Sketch Template

Copyright © mmxx Be Amazing, LLC Publishing Not to be reproduced.

Client Name:

Placement:

Theme:

Planned Date:

Palette

Design:

Details/Notes:

Name _____ Date _____
Forearm Sketch Template

Copyright © mmxx Be Amazing, LLC Publishing. Not to be reproduced.

Client Name:

Placement:

Theme:

Planned Date:

Palette

Design:

Details / Notes:

Name _____   Date _____
Forearm Sketch Template

Copyright © mmxx Be Amazing, LLC Publishing Not to be reproduced.

Client Name:

Placement:

Theme:

Planned Date:

Palette

Design:

Details / Notes:

Copyright © mmxx Be Amazing, LLC Publishing. Not to be reproduced.

Name _____ Date _____
Forearm Sketch Template

Copyright © mmxx Be Amazing, LLC Publishing. Not to be reproduced.

Client Name:

Placement:

Theme:

Planned Date:

Palette

Design:

Details / Notes:

Copyright © mmxx Be Amazing, LLC Publishing. Not to be reproduced.

Name _____ Date _____
Forearm Sketch Template

Copyright © mmxx Be Amazing, LLC Publishing Not to be reproduced.

Client Name:

Placement:

Theme:

Planned Date:

Palette

Design:

Details / Notes:

Copyright © mmxx Be Amazing, LLC Publishing. Not to be reproduced.

Name _____ Date _____
Forearm Sketch Template

Copyright © mmxx Be Amazing, LLC Publishing Not to be reproduced.

Client Name:

Placement:

Theme:

Planned Date:

Palette

Design:

Details / Notes:

Copyright © mmxx Be Amazing. LLC Publishing. Not to be reproduced.

Name _____ Date _____
Forearm Sketch Template

Copyright © mmxx Be Amazing, LLC Publishing. Not to be reproduced.

Client Name:

Placement:

Theme:

Planned Date:

Palette

Design:

Details / Notes:

Copyright © mmxx Be Amazing, LLC Publishing. Not to be reproduced.

Name _____ Date _____
Forearm Sketch Template

Copyright © mmxx Be Amazing, LLC Publishing. Not to be reproduced.

Client Name:

Placement:

Theme:

Planned Date:

Palette

Design:

Details / Notes:

Copyright © mmxx Be Amazing, LLC Publishing. Not to be reproduced.

Name _____ Date _____
Forearm Sketch Template

Copyright © mmxx Be Amazing, LLC Publishing. Not to be reproduced.

Client Name:

Placement:

Theme:

Planned Date:

Palette

Design:

Details / Notes:

Copyright © mmxx Be Amazing, LLC Publishing. Not to be reproduced.

Name _____ Date _____
Forearm Sketch Template

Copyright © mmxx Be Amazing, LLC Publishing. Not to be reproduced.

Client Name:

Placement:

Theme:

Planned Date:

Palette

Design:

Details/Notes:

Copyright © mmxx Be Amazing, LLC Publishing. Not to be reproduced.

Name _____ Date _____
Forearm Sketch Template

Copyright © mmxx Be Amazing, LLC Publishing. Not to be reproduced.

Client Name:

Placement:

Palette

Theme:

Planned Date:

Design:

Details / Notes:

Copyright © mmxx Be Amazing, LLC Publishing. Not to be reproduced.

Name _____ Date _____
Forearm Sketch Template

Copyright © mmxx Be Amazing. LLC Publishing. Not to be reproduced.

Client Name:

Placement:

Theme:

Planned Date:

Palette

Design:

Details / Notes:

Copyright © mmxx Be Amazing, LLC Publishing. Not to be reproduced.

Name _____ Date _____
Forearm Sketch Template

Copyright © mmxx Be Amazing, LLC Publishing. Not to be reproduced.

Client Name:

Placement:

Theme:

Planned Date:

Palette

Design:

Details/Notes:

Copyright © mmxx Be Amazing, LLC Publishing. Not to be reproduced.

Name _____   Date _____
Forearm Sketch Template

Copyright © mmxx Be Amazing, LLC Publishing. Not to be reproduced.

Client Name:

Placement:

Theme:

Planned Date:

Palette

Design:

Details / Notes:

Copyright © mmxx Be Amazing, LLC Publishing. Not to be reproduced.

Name _____ Date _____
Forearm Sketch Template

Copyright © mmxx Be Amazing, LLC Publishing. Not to be reproduced.

Client Name:

Placement:

Theme:

Planned Date:

Palette

Design:

Details / Notes:

Copyright © mmxx Be Amazing, LLC Publishing. Not to be reproduced.

Name _____ Date _____
Forearm Sketch Template

Copyright © mmxx Be Amazing, LLC Publishing. Not to be reproduced.

Client Name:

Placement:

Theme:

Planned Date:

Palette

Design:

Details / Notes:

Copyright © mmxx Be Amazing, LLC Publishing. Not to be reproduced.

Name _____ Date _____
Forearm Sketch Template

Copyright © mmxx Be Amazing, LLC Publishing. Not to be reproduced.

Client Name:

Placement:

Theme:

Planned Date:

Palette

Design:

Details/Notes:

Copyright © mmxx Be Amazing, LLC Publishing. Not to be reproduced.

Name _____ Date _____
Forearm Sketch Template

Copyright © mmxx Be Amazing, LLC Publishing. Not to be reproduced.

Client Name:

Placement:

Theme:

Planned Date:

Palette

Design:

Details / Notes:

Copyright © mmxx Be Amazing, LLC Publishing. Not to be reproduced.

Name _____ Date _____

Forearm Sketch Template

Copyright © mmxx Be Amazing, LLC Publishing. Not to be reproduced.

Client Name:

Placement:

Theme:

Planned Date:

Palette

Design:

Details / Notes:

Copyright © mmxx Be Amazing, LLC Publishing. Not to be reproduced.

Name _____ Date _____

Forearm Sketch Template

Copyright © mmxx Be Amazing, LLC Publishing. Not to be reproduced.

Client Name:

Placement:

Theme:

Planned Date:

Palette

Design:

Details / Notes:

Copyright © mmxx Be Amazing, LLC Publishing. Not to be reproduced.

Name _____ Date _____
Forearm Sketch Template

Copyright © mmxx Be Amazing, LLC Publishing. Not to be reproduced.

Client Name:

Placement:

Theme:

Planned Date:

Palette

Design:

Details / Notes:

Name _____ Date _____
Forearm Sketch Template

Copyright © mmxx Be Amazing, LLC Publishing Not to be reproduced.

Thank You...
...for purchasing our Tattoo Journal and Sketchbook!
Check out other sketchbooks designed
by Tangie Marie and Cameron Purvis.

Blank Comic Sketchbook 200 Bright White Pages
Blank Comic Sketchbook 100 Bright White Pages

Blank Storyboard Sketchbook
Featuring 16:9 Thumbnail Panels 200 Bright White Pages
Blank Storyboard Sketchbook
Featuring 16:9 Thumbnail Panels 100 Bright White Pages

Blank Storyboard Sketchbook
Featuring 4:3 Thumbnail Panels 200 Bright White Pages
Blank Storyboard Sketchbook
Featuring 4:3 Thumbnail Panels 100 Bright White Pages

Blank Storyboard Sketchbook
Featuring 1:1 Thumbnail Panels 200 Bright White Pages
Blank Storyboard Sketchbook
Featuring 1:1 Thumbnail Panels 100 Bright White Pages

Blank Tattoo Journal and Sketchbook
Tattoo Sketchbook and Journal

Need a children's book?
We have those too.
Check out these titles:
Alexander Ant and the Art Contest
Goodnight, Meow
The 12 Nights of Winter

Made in the USA
Coppell, TX
08 May 2022